All About Arrowheads
and Spear Points

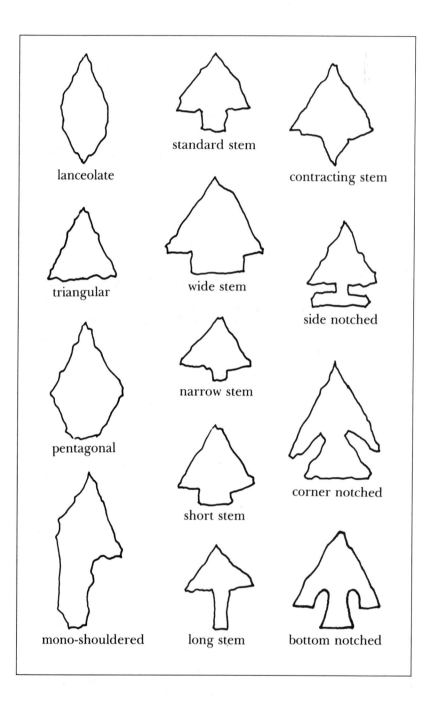

lanceolate

standard stem

contracting stem

triangular

wide stem

side notched

pentagonal

narrow stem

corner notched

short stem

mono-shouldered

long stem

bottom notched

ALL ABOUT

Arrowheads and Spear Points

▶ HOWARD E. SMITH, JR.

Illustrated by
▶ Jennifer Owings Dewey

HENRY HOLT AND COMPANY / NEW YORK

Published by Henry Holt and Company, Inc.,
115 West 18th Street, New York, New York 10011.
Published in Canada by Fitzhenry & Whiteside Limited,
195 Allstate Parkway, Markham, Ontario L3R 4T8.

Library of Congress Cataloging-in-Publication Data
Smith, Howard Everett, 1927–
   All about arrowheads and spear points / by Howard E. Smith, Jr. ;
illustrated by Jennifer Owings Dewey. — 1st ed.
      p. cm.
   Includes index.
   Summary: Describes the different types of arrowheads and spear
points of the Americas, where they may be found, and what they
reveal about the life of ancient peoples.
   ISBN 0-8050-0892-6
   1. Indians of North America—Implements—Juvenile literature.
2. Arrowheads—Juvenile literature.   3. Projectile points—North
America—Juvenile literature.   4. Indians of North America —
Antiquities—Juvenile literature.   5. North America—Antiquities —
Juvenile literature.   [1. Arrowheads.   2. Indians of North
America—Implements.   3. Indians of North America—Antiquities.]
I. Dewey, Jennifer, ill.   II. Title.
E98.I4S63   1989
970.01—dc19   88-39089

First Edition

Printed in the United States of America
10 9 8 7 6 5 4 3 2 1

To John M. Norris,
who makes such a difference
—H.E.S.

▸ Contents

1 ▸ Finding Arrowheads and Spear Points

Someday while you dig in a garden, play in a vacant lot, walk by a creek, or just go for a walk, you might find an ancient arrowhead or spear point. Each year people (many of them children) find thousands of arrowheads and spearheads in all parts of North and South America. These stone points were used by Native Americans (also called Indians), the first of whom had come to the Americas sometime between thirty-three thousand and fifty thousand years ago.

If you want to increase your chances of finding an arrowhead or spear point, look in places where soil has been recently uncovered: in newly plowed fields, along road cuts, and beside or in shallow streams and stream embankments, especially after it has rained.

If you see an arrowhead in your own yard, you may keep it. (Beware! The edges of arrowheads and spearheads are sharp and can cut you.) But always remember that there are places where you may not keep an arrowhead, even though you might be the first to find it. It is against the law to take arrowheads from public lands, especially in national parks and monuments. On lands belonging to private citizens, you must ask permission to keep what you find.

Typically stone arrowheads or spear points had triangular heads. Below that, the stone may have been chipped so that it had a shaft—the narrow "neck" of the stone. But not all arrowheads looked like "typical" ones, so expect surprises. Some lacked shafts. Some were pointed at each end. Some had very oddly shaped shafts.

Spear points and arrowheads could be made only from special stones. Some stones and materials, such as glass, will break in such a way as to produce sharp edges. Only those stones that break or chip this way were used for spear points and arrowheads.

Other types of stone, such as limestone, sandstone, and granite, were not used to make arrowheads and spear points, for no matter how one breaks or tries to chip them, they will never produce a sharp cutting edge.

In short, only special stones were used for making spear points or arrowheads.

One commonly used type of stone is called flint. Flint is a dark-colored quartz. (Most sand grains are made of quartz.) You can recognize flint because it is somewhat glassy in appearance. And like glass its broken edges are sharp. To identify flint, test it. When flint is struck by a piece of steel, such as a file, it will give off sparks.

Other types of stone were also used. Chert is an impure form of flint. Jasper is closely related to chert but is often highly colored. Chalcedony is a type of quartz; it is very smooth and looks waxy. Some chalcedony is transparent, so you can see through it. Obsidian is volcanic glass, usually black in color. Hornfels is a clay that melted deep in the earth, then cooled to become hard. Basalt is similar but blacker. These are just a few of the types of stones that were shaped into sharp-edged, sharp-tipped arrowheads and spearheads that could pierce the hides of animals.

You might find other types of arrowheads made of other materials, such as bone, copper, or iron. In the arctic some were made of walrus or whale ivory. Native Americans also made some of wood. It is very unlikely you will find a wooden arrowhead, for almost all of them rotted away long ago. But if you do see a wooden one, contact your museum or university, as they are very rare and possibly of great scientific value.

Because Native Americans lived throughout the Americas, you can find arrowheads in all the states (except Hawaii), throughout Canada and Mexico, and in Central and South America.

2 ‣ Labeling Your Finds

When you find an arrowhead or spear point, you should write down the exact location of where you found it. For example: "On the bank of Maple Creek, about a mile from the county road #3 bridge," or "At the northeast corner of Mrs. Edwards's garden on Elm St." Be as exact as you can. Also note the date of your find. Write down for example, "Found on January 5, 1989." Describe as carefully as you can the story of your find. Did you find it when it was dug up by a dog? Was it just lying on the surface? Do you suspect that a recent rain uncovered it? If your find was from under the ground, be sure to note how far it was from the surface. Also write down your opinion of why it was there. Was it left from a hunt? Was there possibly a village there?

Someday the information you write down may be valuable. Your find may help archaeologists—scientists who study humans and the way they lived and acted in the past. By digging up the remains of ancient villages, roads, hunting grounds, and the like, archaeologists can learn a great deal about the life of ancient peoples, including Native Americans and their ancestors.

But above all, your find will be of great personal value. When you are older, you can read your notes with pleasure and recall when and where you found your arrowhead or spear point.

The best way to preserve your arrowhead or spear point is to have it wrapped in paper or cushioned in cotton batting or Styrofoam. If you leave several arrowheads or spear points unwrapped in a box where they rattle around, they might chip one another.

Also be careful not to handle them roughly or let them drop. Most are brittle; they can break easily! This is one reason why we so often see broken arrowheads.

It is important to remember that if you believe you've made an important find, get in touch with a local museum or university.

3 ▸ The First Spear Points

No one knows for sure when the first men, women, and children entered the western hemisphere. But the best evidence shows that small hunting groups came from Asia by way of a land bridge across the Bering Strait during the Ice Age. The Ice Age was a period of time when glaciers—constantly melting and reforming—covered much of North America and Europe.

At that time so much seawater had evaporated and

Artist's sketch of an early thrusting spear. This is probably the type of shaft used, but no actual shafts have been found.

fallen as snow, forming glaciers, that the world's sea level was lower than it is now. The level was so low that the Bering Strait, between Alaska and Siberia, had become dry land. In other words, a land bridge connected Asia and North America. Asians crossed it easily and entered North America. But when? Because all the earliest remains are buried, rotted, or lost underwater, no one knows exactly. But it must have been at least thirty-three thousand to possibly fifty thousand years ago.

The earliest groups of people who came into America did not have the weapons of later Native Americans. For example, their spears—if they had any—were merely sharpened wooden shafts.

Tens of thousands of years would pass before the first stone spear points were made. Later, many thousands of years would pass before Native American hunters made bows and arrows.

The history of Native American spear points and arrowheads puzzles experts. It is known that ancient Europeans made stone spear points at least twenty thousand years ago, and that Africans had bows and arrows around ten to twelve thousand years ago. Yet Native Americans did not at that time know of the invention of either spear points or bows and arrows. No one knows why this is so, but it was probably just a matter of distance. Europe and Africa were very remote, and Native Americans did not know such places existed.

At any rate, Native Americans first had wooden spears with fire-hardened tips, then eventually invented the stone spear point on their own and, much later, the bow and arrow.

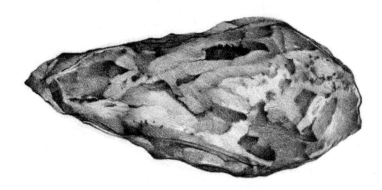

The lanceolate point was first found in Venezuela. It is the earliest known point in all of the Americas.

The oldest known stone spear point in all of the Americas was found in Venezuela. It is about fourteen thousand years old. It is called a lanceolate point. (Lanceolate means "shaped like a little lance.") Both ends tapered to similarly shaped and sized points.

Apparently, Native Americans other than those in Venezuela learned how to make and use this type of spear point. The techniques of how to make and use it spread from tribe to tribe. After many centuries passed, the knowledge spread northward by way of Central America and Mexico to those Native Americans who lived in today's United States.

Hunters used this kind of spear point against big game. We know this because, as we'll see later on, such points have been found imbedded in the bones of large, prehistoric mammals.

It surprises many people that such a small, two-inch-long point could kill an animal—especially large, powerful animals such as prehistoric giant bison and mammoths. Yet points like these did. To understand this, let us think about how a spear point works. It works because of the pressure on the point. If a 150-pound man pushed with all his weight on such a spear, the tip of the spear point would have all 150 pounds of his weight focused on a very, very small area. The area of the point of the spear might be only 1/100th of a square inch. If so, that means the pressure at the tip is tremendous—15,000 pounds per square inch! The sharper the point was, the greater its pressure and penetration would have been.

Once in its target, a spear point would wound an animal. Hunters would then follow the animal, or the trail it left, for hours, even days, until it dropped from loss of blood. Sometimes a well-thrown spear would kill a large animal immediately. Either way, the spear was a deadly and effective weapon.

Thanks to the spear point, hungry men and women did not die of starvation. From animals they also got hides for clothing and shelters; sinews for thread; and bones for tools.

We should remember that spear points that may look primitive to us meant life to people long ago. Spear points were as important to them as modern tractors, plows, and fertilizers are to us.

Of all humankind's inventions, the spear was one of the most important. It gave humans on all continents power over all animals, even the largest. It greatly expanded the food supplies of the entire world. Everyone's ancestors used it. In fact, spears with stone points were so effective that they were used in Australia and New Guinea even into the twentieth century. If it had not been for spear points, few if any of us would be alive today.

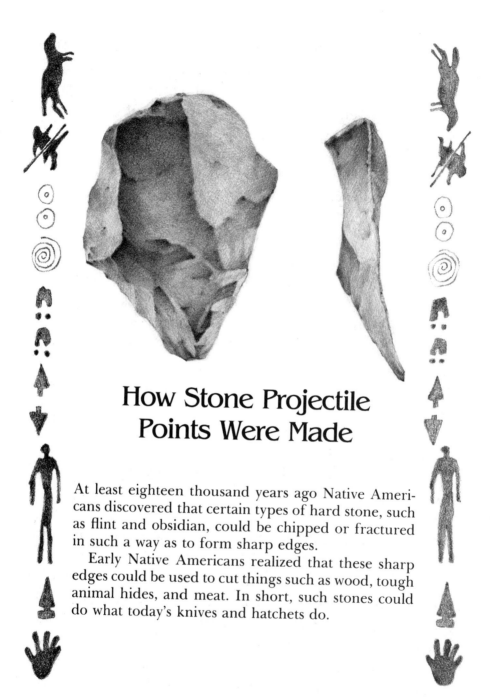

How Stone Projectile
Points Were Made

At least eighteen thousand years ago Native Americans discovered that certain types of hard stone, such
as flint and obsidian, could be chipped or fractured
in such a way as to form sharp edges.

Early Native Americans realized that these sharp
edges could be used to cut things such as wood, tough
animal hides, and meat. In short, such stones could
do what today's knives and hatchets do.

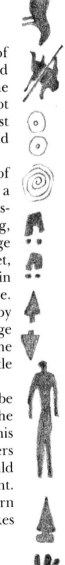

The Native Americans used several methods of shaping stone into tools. One technique that they used is called pressure pointing. A stone was held by one hand in leather so that the worker's hand would not be cut. A piece of wood or bone was pressed against a broken edge of the stone, and a small flake would break off that would have a sharp edge.

Another method of applying pressure to a piece of flint or other suitable type of stone was to make a breastplate of hard wood. A man would apply pressure to the stone using the breastplate and a long, attached rod. He would hold the rod against the edge of the stone, which was often held between his feet, and press hard against the edge of the stone. Again a flake would break off that would have a sharp edge.

It was also possible to break flakes off a stone by holding the stone in leather and then striking the edge with a wooden stick called a baton. Sometimes the Native Americans would use the flakes, with very little shaping, for their spear points and arrowheads.

But most spear points and arrowheads had to be further shaped after a flake was obtained. Usually the worker would hold the partly shaped point in his hand, which was protected by leather. In his fingers he would hold a small pointed baton, which he would then hit with a rock against the edge of the point. This method, which was similar to the way a modern hammer and chisel works, would produce small flakes and eventually a usable, sharp tool.

Spears were important to early humans not only for hunting but also for protection.

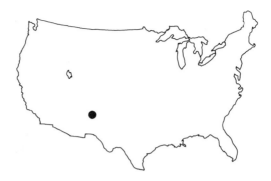

4 ▸ The Sandia Point

Sandia points were odd-shaped spear points. They had a shaft that extended down from one side of the point. Such a point is called a mono-shouldered point. These unusual and rare points are found mainly in the Southwest, especially in New Mexico.

Sandia spear points, the oldest ever found in the United States or Canada, were found in a cave located in the Sandia Mountains, east of Albuquerque, New Mexico. The cave is now called Sandia Cave.

Before this discovery it was known that Native Americans had used the cave as a shelter. Then in 1936 Dr. Frank Hibben, an archaeologist, thinking that old finds might lie in the dust of the floor, began to dig inside the long, narrow cave.

On the floor of the cave lay deep layers of dirt that

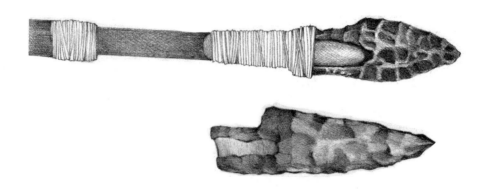

The Sandia point was first found in New Mexico. Notice the mono-shouldered shaft that extends down one side of the point.

had been there for thousands of years. Hibben and his helpers dug down into it. When they came to a lower level, they found the remains of ancient camp fires. They also found very old spear points called Folsom points. (We will learn much more about them later on.)

Though the Folsom points were a major find, Dr. Hibben felt that deeper down there might possibly lie even older points. He and his helpers continued the hard, dusty work. Eventually their efforts paid off.

They came across a type of stone spear point that had never been seen by scientists. It was extremely ancient. No one knew how old it was, but scientists determined—by the depths of the dirt on the floor of the cave and other evidence—that it must have been made about ten thousand years ago.

With the point were the bones of prehistoric animals, among them mastodons, now-extinct camels of America, and mammoths.

The discovery in 1936 of the Sandia point—the oldest spear point in America—stunned the world, for it showed that men, women, and children had been in North America for at least ten thousand years.

Today the country around Sandia Cave is semidesert covered with scattered piñon pines, juniper trees, sage, and yucca plants. But when people lived in the cave, the climate was a bit wetter. Big trees, probably ponderosa pines, grew there. Rivers and streams were fuller. Herds of giant bison, deer, mammoths, and camels were commonly seen. In addition, giant sloths roamed about in the forests.

As for the native Sandia Cave people, we know almost nothing about them. None of their bones have been found. We do not know what they looked like, how they dressed, or what language they spoke. All we know is that they were great hunters.

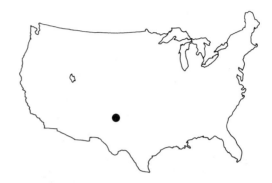

5 ▸ The Clovis Point

Clovis points were almost always made of chipped chalcedony, jasper, or chert. These stones are much like flint —hard, brittle, and easy to chip. Clovis points were usually about two and a quarter to four and a half inches long. In most cases they were about a third as wide as they were long.

These points were used mainly to kill enormous animals, namely mammoths. We know this because mammoth bones are almost always found near Clovis points. Some points have even been found still stuck in mammoth bones!

The spear points found in Sandia Cave and at first called Sandia points were later renamed Clovis points by scientists. This is because far better examples of this type of spear point were found near, and named after, Clovis, New Mexico.

Though we know nothing about the people who lived in Sandia Cave, we know much more about many other Native Americans who hunted with Clovis points.

Since most Clovis points and mammoth bones that have been found together were near or in places that were once shallow lakes or bogs, experts are sure that mammoths were hunted in such places. Apparently the hunters waited for huge mammoths and mastodons to come to the ponds to drink. When these heavy animals walked into the deep mud, their feet sank down into it, making it impossible for them to run away from hunters. Then men attacked them with spears. They probably attacked the female mammoths most often, because they were smaller and less dangerous than the big males. Before the mammoths or mastodons could run away, spears had either wounded them or killed them. (It is interesting that prehistoric Africans using spears hunted animals

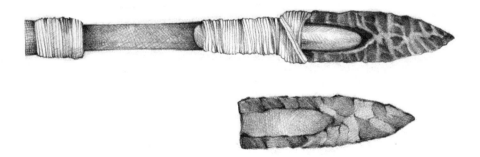

Clovis points, usually about two and a quarter to four and a half inches long, were often used to kill enormous animals such as mammoths.

such as zebras, antelope, and elephants at water holes in the same way. Some African tribes continued to hunt with bows and arrows into the twentieth century.)

Perhaps at times the hunters herded the mammoths into the mud. Perhaps—and it is just a guess—men frightened them with flaming torches. The terrified beasts would have run from the flames into the deep mud and become trapped.

Mammoth and mastodon hides were thick and tough. Even a strong man could not throw a spear with enough speed to pierce their hides. We know from the shape and weight of the points that the spears must have been light-weight. How could men throw such lightweight spears into such large animals?

To increase the speed of the spear, the hunters made throwing sticks. One can understand how a throwing stick works by placing a piece of tightly wadded-up paper on the end of a yardstick and throwing it by swinging the yardstick over the shoulder. The wadded-up paper will move far faster than it would if thrown without the yard-stick.

In a similar manner Native Americans made and used a type of throwing stick called an atlatl (pronounced *ott*-lot-ul).

Atlatls were flat throwing sticks. To use one, a hunter rested the spear on the flat surface. A knob at the end of the atlatl held the end of the spear but did not grip it. To throw the spear, the hunter swung the throwing stick in an overhand motion, over his shoulder. At the top of the atlatl's arc, when it was moving at its fastest,

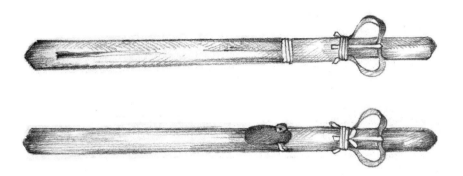

Atlatls. These flat throwing sticks were used to throw spears up to a hundred and fifty miles per hour.

the spear flew away from it. A spear could reach a speed of over a hundred and fifty miles per hour.

Such a fast-moving, lightweight spear with a sharp stone point was an effective weapon. The point would go through even the tough hide of a mammoth. It was a great improvement on heavier, hand-thrown spears.

The Clovis point people, as they are called, lived in fairly large groups. On the American plains they often lived in hutlike shelters on small hills or sometimes dunes. The small huts were usually placed in a semicircle. It is believed that the people moved with the game herds, hunting them all year around. Scientists believe this because unlike any other points, Clovis points have been found in almost all the states of the United States.

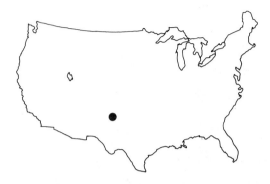

6 ▸ The Folsom Point

The Folsom stone spear point was unlike any other in the world. It was only about two and a half inches long. The tip was sharp, and at the base were two small projections on each side. Nothing like it had ever been seen before. It was found over a very wide area, but mainly in the great plains just east of the Rocky Mountains.

The most interesting and unusual feature of the spear point was that it had a wide groove running from the base almost to the tip on each side of the point. No one is sure what these grooves were for. Either they were used to secure the spear point to a wooden shaft, examples of which have long ago rotted away, or the groove was made for the purpose of keeping a wound open so that an animal would bleed to death quickly.

Of all the finds of Native American stone spear points,

none was as important to our understanding of Native Americans as the discovery of the Folsom point.

In the 1920s, a cowboy named George McJunken was riding his horse on the Crowfoot Ranch. All around him lay the vast, lonely plains of northeastern New Mexico. The nearest town, Folsom, New Mexico, was far away.

As he rode in an arroyo (a western name for a dry riverbed), some bones sticking out of the steep embankment caught his attention. He got off his horse and examined them. He had seen many bones before, but these were unlike any he knew of.

He believed they were prehistoric. Not only were they unfamiliar, but they lay under many feet of dirt. Such layers of dirt could cover the bones only over thousands of years of time.

He told Carl Schwachheim, a teacher at Raton, New Mexico, of his find. Schwachheim said he would look at the site. Unfortunately Mr. McJunken would never know the importance of his find, for he died in 1925, two years before Schwachheim could get to the site. When Schwachheim finally saw the bones, he realized that they had to be those of prehistoric animals. Schwachheim soon notified the Denver Museum of Natural History. During 1926, 1927, and all through 1928–29 archaeologists from the museum dug at the site. They soon realized that most of the bones were those of a giant bison. The most remarkable thing about the giant bison was that the last ones had become extinct some ten thousand years ago.

Then another amazing discovery was made. A rib bone of the giant bison was found, and stuck right into the bone itself was a spear point.

Once the spear point was found, archaeologists from all over America and from many foreign countries came to see the site.

All who saw the stone spear point in the rib agreed that the giant bison had been killed by Native Americans during prehistoric times. The evidence was overwhelming. After careful studies it was determined that the point was between nine thousand and ten thousand years old.

The fact that a spear point lay embedded in the bones of a prehistoric animal of such age shocked many experts. It proved beyond a reasonable doubt that Native Americans had been in America far longer than anyone had previously thought possible.

Until the discovery most historians, archaeologists, anthropologists, and other experts were quite certain that the Americas had been uninhabited by humans until about fifteen hundred years ago. They reasoned from the Aztec and Mayan ruins that groups of people familiar with European and ancient Egyptian and Chinese cultures had been the first to come into America. Otherwise, thought the experts, how would they know how pyramids, such as the ones Mayans had constructed, were built? And how would Native Americans have known how to build the huge mounds in the Ohio Valley?

In addition, the experts knew that the mounds in the Ohio Valley had been built in historic times and were only a few hundred years old. All evidence had pointed to the conclusion that the Native Americans had been in North America for only fifteen hundred years at the most! But the spear point stuck in the rib of a prehistoric bison changed all that. The point proved that Native

The Folsom point has a wide groove running from the base almost to the tip on each side of the point.

Americans had been here at least ten thousand years.

After the original Folsom point was found, many others were found: in Sandia Cave; in Lubbock and Midland, Texas; in Lindenmeier, Colorado; and in MacHaffie, Montana. These sites show that the Folsom people lived and hunted mostly on the plains.

These finds gave us a glimpse into the lives of the people we call the Folsom people.

We know, for example, how the men, probably with the help of women and children, hunted big game such as the now-extinct giant bison and mammoths.

The hunters found narrow, deep, steep-sided arroyos that ended in a steep-sided embankment. Somehow the hunters forced the big game into such an arroyo. It is believed that the hunters, and maybe also women and children, chased the animals into it by running with flaming torches, by waving hide blankets, and by hollering at them.

Once the animals were in the arroyo, they could not get out of it without running by hunters who were already hidden in and above it. Once the animals were trapped, the men easily speared them.

Several camps of Folsom people have been discovered. Oddly enough, they were usually not near such arroyos but instead were near large, shallow lakes or beaver-pond-studded meadows. Perhaps they also hunted big game by chasing animals into mud, where they would get stuck. And if the animals did not become stuck in the mud, they sank far enough into it so that they could not run fast. It is also possible that Folsom people didn't hunt big game at the lakes. Perhaps instead they hunted the birds and other small animals that went there.

We know that the Folsom people cured skins because stone hide scrapers have been found. Stone scrapers were used to scrape off fat and meat from the insides of hides so that the hides could be properly cured. Scrapers are an old tool and were also used in prehistoric Africa, Europe, and Asia, as were stone knives for skinning animals, stone drills, and stone choppers for cutting wood. Scientists have used stone knives to skin animals and reported that they worked just about as well as modern steel knives.

Stone scrapers were used to scrape off fat and meat from the insides of animal hides so that the hides could be properly cured.

Another find was particularly fascinating. Flat stones were found with powdered rock pigments on them. This suggests that the Folsom people used the stones as palettes and painted on the hide covers of their shelters, or on rocks, wood, or perhaps their own bodies.

We know something else, too. Studies have shown that the Folsom people were wise in hunting large animals such as mammoths and giant bison. Though large animals were harder to hunt than small animals and also more dangerous, the hunters got much more food for their efforts than if they had spent more time hunting antelope, birds, or any medium-size or small animals.

A large mammoth no doubt fed groups of Folsom people for days and perhaps for weeks, especially if they cured the meat with smoke.

It is believed that the hunters, after making a big kill, gave offerings and thankful prayers to the killed animals. Within the last hundred years members of the Pueblo tribes and other Native Americans offered such prayers to the killed animals of the hunt, and it is reasonable to believe that they were following an ancient tradition.

After feasting, the people probably spent days telling stories, singing, dancing, celebrating their religion, or just joking and playing games.

Yet they probably did not live solely on the meat of big game. During the spring, summer, and autumn, women and children most likely gathered nuts, berries, fruits, and roots to eat.

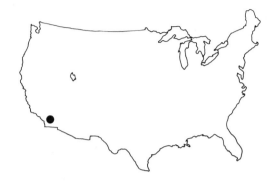

7 ▸ The First Bows and Arrows

If you find stone projectile points that are smaller than the spear points we've seen, they were almost undoubtedly arrowheads. Size alone identifies arrowheads.

Arrowheads, of course, were on arrows shot from bows. Until now we haven't mentioned either arrowheads or bows and arrows. This is because the earliest weapons of the Native Americans were spears. But in time Native Americans developed bows and arrows.

When did they first use bows and arrows? No one knows the exact answer to this question. But some early

The earliest arrows did not have feathers.

finds indicate that the Native Americans used them at least three thousand years ago. Archaeologists digging in La Jolla, California, found some stone points that were smaller than stone spear points. Because of the sharp points and the size of the stones, scientists are almost positive that they were the tips of some of the first arrows shot with bows.

The Native Americans of La Jolla lived in a marvelous climate. They had plenty to eat, and life might have been relatively easy. Oak trees produced nutritionally rich acorns. In the forests deer, birds, and many other animals could be hunted. On the seashore at La Jolla the people could find clams, mussels, and abalones. They could catch many types of fish in the ocean. Moreover, the climate was gentle. Because California seemed so ideal, there was a large population of Native Americans living there.

Stone points found at La Jolla date back as far as three thousand years. Scientists don't know whether these points were arrowheads or spearheads because their size does not make it clear. They were not as big as some spear points and not as small as some arrowheads, so it is difficult to say exactly what these points were.

Since wooden remains of two-thousand-year-old bows and arrows have been found, it is easy for scientists to say that the two-thousand-year-old points belonged to arrows and not spears. But since similar wooden remains of three-thousand-year-old weapons have not been found, scientists are not sure whether the three-thousand-year-old points were arrowheads or spear points. At any rate, it is clear that the Native Americans of La Jolla used bows and arrows at least two thousand years ago.

Africans who had migrated into Europe had bows and arrows at least ten to twelve thousand years ago. This is known from their ancient rock drawings, which depict hunters who held bows and arrows in their hands.

But does that prove that the idea of bows and arrows went from one group of peoples to another all the way across Europe, Asia, and into America? Not really. If that had happened, the remains of bows and arrows would have undoubtedly shown up thousands of years earlier in America. But, in fact, no such early remains have shown up!

Since there is such a huge time lag between the estimated date of European arrowheads and the first American ones, it is unlikely that Europeans passed on their discovery to the Americans. Scientists believe instead that the isolated Native Americans, who knew nothing of Europe, invented the bow and arrow on their own. Scientists believe that it was invented by California natives in particular.

Those earliest arrows, used by the natives of La Jolla, did not have feathers on them. Tests done with La Jolla arrowheads prove this. A featherless arrow can be used only with a heavier-than-usual arrowhead. The bowman must aim his featherless arrow high so that it will move upward at a steep angle and then arc down on the target. Such an arrow is not nearly as effective as a feathered arrow with a smaller arrowhead.

A feathered arrow can be shot more directly at a target than can a featherless arrow. It is far easier to aim. Moreover, it hits with a greater impact, so the arrow can penetrate more deeply. However, as we will see, centuries would pass before any Native Americans had feathered arrows.

Soon after the La Jolla natives had bows and arrows, people of the Great Basin and desert regions of today's Four Corners area, where Colorado, Utah, Arizona, and New Mexico meet, had them. The people there may have reinvented the bow and arrow on their own. But it is more likely that they got the idea from California natives.

Slowly but surely the use of the bow and arrow spread across both North and South America. It had proved itself as a good hunting weapon and would be used until long after Europeans arrived on American shores and even after pioneers had settled in the West.

8 ‣ Inuit Ivory Points

In the arctic one can find ivory spear and harpoon points, and also ivory arrowheads. Though people think true ivory comes only from elephant tusks, the hard material from the teeth of whales and tusks of walruses is also a type of ivory. In the arctic, Inuits, also called Eskimos, used it for many things, including projectile points on hunting weapons. The ivory of whales and walruses is white and hard. But it is not nearly as hard as flint. Old ivory turns a soft, off-white color, barely tinted brown with age. Only in the arctic will you find such ivory points.

To understand why the Inuits used ivory, a softer material than stone, we should consider the arctic landscape. The arctic is the huge area that surrounds the Arctic

Ocean. Most peoples of the arctic lived near the coastline, which is tens of thousands of miles long.

Often snow and ice covered much of the shore, making it hard to find flint or any other rocks. However, walruses and whales could be hunted all year long. Their teeth and tusks could be carved into tools. Since ivory was common and fairly easy to get, it is natural that the peoples of the arctic would use it for tools such as spear points and arrowheads.

People have lived in the arctic for many thousands of years, but they have lived in Asia possibly as long as a hundred thousand years. Arctic-dwelling people in Asia have used ivory for tools for many thousands of years—perhaps for all those years.

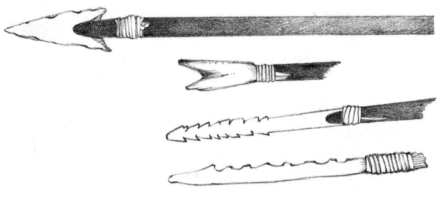

In the arctic, Inuits used ivory to make projectile points for hunting weapons.

Though early wanderers entered North America by arctic routes, mainly the Bering Strait, about thirty-three thousand years ago and perhaps much, much earlier, the first Americans were not Inuits.

Inuits hunted with harpoons and spears. Unlike those of spears, the wooden shafts of harpoons fell off after striking their target.

Inuits followed much later. In fact, it is likely that they were the *last* group to have migrated here from Asia. They arrived with a fully developed Euro-Asian culture, that was not at all primitive. The Inuits, after leaving Asia, probably arrived in North America about A.D. 1000, only a thousand years ago. In fact, they did not appear in Greenland until the 1400s.

We know quite a bit about ancient ivory arrowheads and spear points of the early Inuits. One of the best-preserved finds in all of North America was an Inuit house that was almost intact. It was found in Utqiagvik, near Barrow, Alaska. About five hundred years ago an ice slide crushed the house and killed the family in it. Clothing, stored food, timbers of the house, and many ivory utensils were found perfectly preserved by the ice and cold. Among them were beautifully carved ivory arrowheads, spear points, and harpoon heads.

It is easy to mistake a harpoon for a spear. At first glance they look alike, but actually they are quite different. Harpoons were, and still are on occasion, used for hunting marine mammals such as seals and walruses and in some rare instances whales. Therefore their design was different from spears, which were used to hunt land animals.

In many ways a harpoon did resemble a spear: A man threw it; the point pierced the side of an animal; barbs on the point held it in so that it would not come out.

But a harpoon, unlike a spear, was made so that the wooden shaft of the harpoon fell off after it struck its target. It usually floated away, never to be used again. The point, however, stayed in the animal. Attached to the point was a long line. At the end of the line there were air bags, usually made of seal bladders.

Once hit, the mammal dived, often to great depths. As it dived, it pulled the air bags after it. The bags slowed the animal's dive, which greatly tired the animal. The bags also helped the hunters to follow the hidden animal underwater because they could see the air bags on the surface.

A mammal, such as a seal, whale, or walrus, must come to the surface of the water to breathe. When it did, a hunter in a fast kayak could chase it and harpoon it again.

When the animal finally tired from pulling the air bags

and from losing blood, it gave up the struggle. Then the hunter killed it with a special knife or spear.

Inuits also used bows and arrows with ivory arrowheads. Ivory arrowheads and spearheads are often thinner than stone arrowheads and spearheads. Usually they have barbs. An arrow or spear may have two or three ivory points.

The Inuits lived in the coldest, bleakest area of North America. Yet they learned how to survive in the arctic. They invented the igloo and created snow goggles to protect their eyes from glare. They crafted marvelously tailored fur clothing, and tools, art objects, and utensils considered by archaeologists to be among the most ingenious and fascinating artifacts in all the Americas.

9 ▸ Copper Points

If you live near the Great Lakes and nearby regions all the way through New York State and Ohio, you might find old spear points, usually about nine inches long, made of copper. Copper is a reddish-colored metal. Pennies are made of copper and tin. The most common electrical wires are made of copper. When old, it blackens and often turns green. (Greenish rocks or green stains on rocks may indicate copper ore.)

Native Americans used the copper spear points mainly to hunt deer and elk. The copper spear points were made

Copper points from the Great Lakes region were made long before anyone else knew how to use metals.

long, long before white settlers traded metal objects with Native Americans. In fact, the Great Lakes copper points are so old, some having been used seventy-four hundred years ago, that they were made before anyone else on earth knew how to use metals.

But how could that have been? How could they have made copper spear points before the metal age even began? This came about because of a geologic oddity. About a billion years ago volcanic mountains rose in the regions where the Great Lakes are found today. As molten rocks came up, so did pure, melted copper. The lava cooled, and so did the copper. The pure copper remained in the ground even after the mountains had eroded away. It was a very unusual event.

About seventy-four hundred years ago Native Americans found this pure copper. Intrigued by it, they began to make things out of it, mostly for trade with other tribes. They soon discovered that it was a marvelous material. They pounded it into sheets, from which they cut knives and spear points. They also cut from the sheets such things as fishhooks, pins, bracelets, ornaments, and odd, crescent-shaped objects that were probably knives. Also mostly for trade, they made rings from rolled copper sheets. Uncut sheets of copper were traded far and wide.

The first people to use copper like this were part of a larger culture that extended from northern New York all the way to eastern North Dakota, and from Lake Winnipeg in today's Canada all the way south to Chicago. It included all the Great Lakes. This region was heavily populated compared to other parts of North America.

Across the entire area, people of the copper-point culture shared the same way of life and the same types of goods.

Not only did the Native Americans there use copper, but they used many of the other resources of the region. They used shells and stones for various tools and implements. From various fibers made of basswood bark or nettle vines, for example, they made rope and string, which they used for many purposes. They made moccasins and sandals of leather and other materials. Theirs was one of the richest of all North American cultures.

The old copper-point culture, after existing for a great length of time, some thirty-five hundred years, slowly faded away. After about a thousand years ago, when the Cahokia of Illinois last used copper objects in burials, the Native Americans discontinued their use of copper. The Mayans of Mexico and the Incas of South America, however, became very sophisticated in their use of metals, developing methods to melt them down and pour them into forms.

So the old copper-point culture was forgotten by the descendants of the old copper-point men and women, and it disappeared. Once more they began making stone spear points and arrowheads.

Even though the old copper-point culture disappeared from the Great Lakes region, the remaining people still thrived. Eventually they invented the birchbark canoe. (Some people think these canoes were, and still are, the best boats in the world for lakes and rapids.) They had toboggans and made crude pottery. The old copper-point culture evolved into the woodlands culture, which became based more and more on agriculture. The woodlands natives grew corn, squash, beans, and tobacco. The woodlands culture existed from thirty-five hundred years ago into the last century.

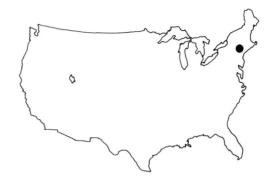

10 ▸ The Deer Hunters

Most stone arrowheads in the eastern part of the United States have a triangular head, a shaft, and a notched base. These arrowheads are made of flint or other similar

Typical northeastern arrowheads and arrow. Feathers placed near the end of an arrow help guide its flight and make its penetrating power greater.

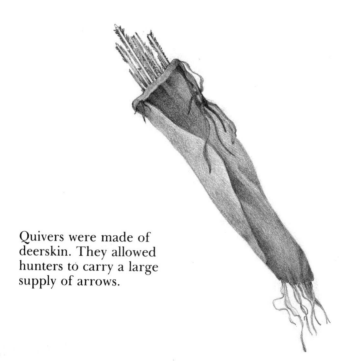

Quivers were made of deerskin. They allowed hunters to carry a large supply of arrows.

stones. These are familiar to us, for their shape is used on many of today's forest signs and trails.

We saw earlier that bows and arrows appeared in the West. But the arrows did not have feathers. Because they did not, it was difficult to shoot the arrow accurately, especially over long distances.

We also saw how feathers placed near the end of an arrow help guide its flight and make its penetrating power greater.

About eleven hundred years ago Native Americans placed the first feathers on arrows. Today we call those Native Americans the deer hunters. Of course, Native Americans hunted deer wherever deer could be found, but few could count on killing a steady supply of them.

With feathered arrows all that changed. Once he had feathered arrows, a skilled hunter in the forested lands of the Northeast, where deer were most common, could almost always get enough deer to feed and clothe his family. Feathered arrows gave the eastern woodlands Native Americans a sure supply of food, as well as skins for clothing and moccasins.

Native Americans hunted deer with feathered arrows. They used deer hides for clothing, tepees, tools, and weapons.

The addition of feathers to arrows was such a success that other tribes beyond the forests began making feathered arrows. The invention eventually spread to Native Americans in all the Americas, from the most northern arctic coast almost to Cape Horn in South America.

The deer hunters helped the first colonists—especially those of Massachusetts, New York, and other northeastern colonies—to survive. They taught them how to grow corn, make snowshoes, and find edible plants, and aided them in many other ways. We know their names from history books: Iroquois, Algonquin, Massachusetts, Wampanoag, Powhatan, and others.

The native peoples used deerskins for women's dresses and men's leggings, and bark for wigwams and canoes. They also made snowshoes and toboggans. They invented the game lacrosse.

The feathered arrow was a potent weapon. Using it, they won many early battles against European explorers and against other invaders.

Many Native Americans actually preferred arrows to bullets. Arrows had one great advantage: They were silent. Noisy guns jammed often, and when they did fire, they scared away game animals or warned enemies.

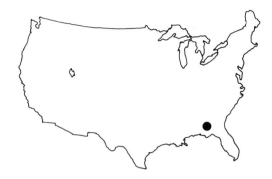

11 ▸ Bird Points

As we have seen, most arrowheads are made so that they have a sharp point. But you might find some stone arrowheads that do not have sharp points. A sharp point pierces a vital organ such as the heart and kills the animal. But Native Americans did not always want to do that. This was especially true when they hunted birds. Birds have small, hollow bones. A pointed arrowhead can easily shatter these frail bones so that the meat of the bird is filled with tiny bone fragments. If that happens, a person cannot eat the bird. Consequently the Native Americans learned to make blunt arrowheads that would not penetrate the bird's flesh. These arrows had either no arrowhead at all or small, blunt, stone heads, which are also called bunts. When such an arrow hit a bird, it stunned it so that the bird would fall helplessly to the ground. The hunter could pick up the helpless bird, kill it without ruining the meat, and take it back to camp for food. If you find a bunt arrowhead, it was probably a bird point.

Native Americans of the Southeast, and in other widely scattered areas, used such blunt arrowheads.

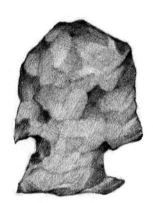

Blunt arrowheads were used to hunt birds because pointed arrowheads shattered bones and ruined the meat.

We know more about the sixteenth-century life style of the inhabitants of the southeastern United States than about any other Native Americans. An artist and explorer named John White drew pictures of them during the years 1585–93. They were some of the earliest European pictures of Native Americans in action.

Southeastern natives for the most part lived in small cities. Nearby were large fields that belonged to the women who tended them. Each year there was a great ceremony to celebrate the first corn harvest. Every fire in the village was put out, and people performed cleansing ceremonies. Then new fires were lit—not such an easy chore in those days, when fires were started with wooden drills.

The city was ruled by a chief. Big cities, such as those

of the Natchez, were ruled by kings. The kings were carried about on chairs supported by servants. So were the kings' wives. A kingship did not pass from king to son, or prince. Kings were chosen for their wisdom and leadership abilities.

Often at the center of a city was a high mound on top of which was a small temple. In all cities there was a public square, and near it a solidly built council house. These houses were much sturdier and more permanent than wigwams or teepees.

Though the women owned land and worked in the fields, the men lived for warfare. The warriors constantly raided other cities for goods, slaves, and above all for prisoners.

We know from White's and others' pictures and evidence that the men of the Southeast used very long bows that were slightly longer than the men were tall. Short bows, which were often used for bird hunting, were easy to carry and were used later, mostly by Native Americans who had horses. When hunting most animals or enemies, they used pointed arrowheads, but for birds they used the blunt arrowheads.

12 ▸ Polished Stone Points

If you live near the seacoast in the Northwest from parts of Washington to parts of Alaska, you might find polished stone spear points that were *not* shaped by being chipped. Instead, though made of stone (usually hard slate, dense granite, or porphyry, a type of granite), they were smooth and had smooth edges. Native Americans ground them into shape by using sandstone and other stones. Such stone points are called polished stones. Some were brought to a beautiful, shiny, high polish.

It is believed that the Northwest Native Americans did

Polished stone points were not chipped or flaked. Their surfaces were smooth, and they had smooth edges.

not use these polished spear points and arrowheads for hunting purposes—they would not have worked as well as flaked points. Also, they took hours of work to make, and a hunter could not afford to lose such valuable points, as he surely would, during a hunt.

Apparently the Northwest natives used the polished points for ceremonial and religious purposes. The Northwest peoples, unlike many natives, had a great deal of wealth. They made large wooden houses out of cut lumber. They owned finely made boxes, and had a wide assortment of tools and implements. They had more than enough to eat. They hunted whales from huge, sixty-foot-long boats. They caught cod and other big sea fish. They caught large supplies of salmon in rivers. They had nuts and berries from the forests. They hunted deer, bear, and mountain goats.

With such wealth they had time for leisure and for extraordinary ceremonies. Enormous wealth, such as large canoes, furs, fish oils, and slaves, was displayed. Men dressed in bear skins danced. Odd, frightening masks were worn that opened up to show other masks. Many natives belonged to secret societies, and sang and danced to the sound of drums and rattles. It is more than likely that the polished stone points were used somehow in these wondrous ceremonies.

Other Native Americans besides the Northwest natives made polished stone points. Many of these points have been found in the Southwest, for example, where again they were probably used in ceremonies.

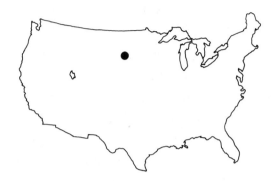

13 ▸ Iron Arrowheads and Spear Points

When explorers from Europe arrived in North America during the early 1500s, they found that the Native Americans used only stone, wood, bone, antler tips, or ivory for their spear points, arrowheads, and harpoons. (The old copper points had been long forgotten by then.)

The explorers brought things new to the Native Americans, such as glass beads, woven blankets, and metal cooking pots. But above all they brought with them metal tools and weapons, which the natives had never seen before.

The explorers quickly traded iron goods for furs. Among those things traded were the famous tomahawks. But lesser known were the iron arrowheads and spear points. Thousands were traded. Across parts of the continent a few might still be found, mostly encrusted with rust.

The iron spear point, in particular, is of interest. During the early and middle 1800s, painters such as George Catlin and Karl Bodmer went to visit the natives of the plains, among them the Sioux, Mandan, Crow, and Blackfoot. The artists were naturally fascinated to see Native Americans on horseback ride up to the huge bison and kill them with steel-pointed lances.

In actuality, most of the bison killed from the early 1800s on by Native Americans were not killed by steel-pointed lances but by steel-pointed arrowheads. Later Native Americans used guns.

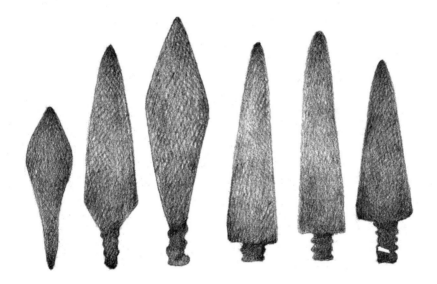

Iron arrowheads and spear points were traded to Native Americans by early explorers.

The last iron arrowheads were used in the late 1800s. They were used, for example, in fights with the U.S. Cavalry. The most famous example of a fight occurred when Native Americans charged American troops under General Custer in the Battle of the Little Bighorn, June 25, 1876. Though most native warriors had the very latest repeating rifles, most preferred to use their bows and arrows in the battle. During that battle, which is also called Custer's Last Stand, all the American troops, including Custer, were killed by Sioux and Cheyenne warriors.

By 1900 no arrowheads or spear points were used by any Native Americans or Canadians south of the Arctic.

On the other hand, Inuits in the frozen northlands continued to use arrowheads, spear points, and, above all, harpoons into the twentieth century. In fact, a few of them still use such arrowheads and harpoon points today.

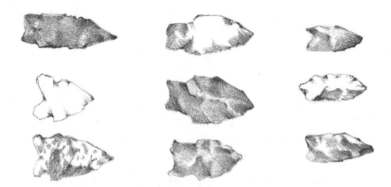

14 ▸ Conclusion

Through the development of effective weapons and tools, Native Americans were able to survive in an often harsh and brutal climate for thousands of years.

The invention of the bow and arrow, the spear, scraping knives, and other stone tools, and the skills required to make them, were tremendously impressive. In fact, it has been found that those stone implements were as efficient as today's knives and other steel tools.

The major advantage of modern equipment is that it is more durable. Since steel is not brittle like stone is, modern tools will generally outlast those made of stone. But in terms of quality, design, and craftmanship, the work of Native Americans was unique and sophisticated.

Native Americans developed or discovered a number of things that we still use today—and probably take for granted. Vegetables such as potatoes, corn, and yams were cultivated by Native Americans. And without their ingenuity, we would be without the important ingredients for a cup of hot chocolate or a vanilla ice-cream cone. Also, clothing and sports equipment would not be the same—Native Americans designed and made the first parkas, snowshoes, and canoes.

Most of the Native Americans' culture has now been destroyed; their way of life is gone forever. So more than just learning about the things we have inherited from the Native Americans, we must learn to recognize the dignity and achievement of their vanished culture. That is why finding, preserving, and studying Native American artifacts like arrowheads and spear points is not only interesting but very important. Each small stone is a piece of history. Each one can help you understand and appreciate the life of the very first Americans.

Index

Page numbers in *italics* indicate illustrations.